Suck It Up, Buttercup

10 Tough-Love Strategies To Get You Off Your Butt and Making Money

Contents

Foreword

When I was asked to write the Foreword for this book, I thought to myself "I'm not gonna say what a big deal it is, because everyone says that." But, guess what? Now, that I'm actually doing it, I realize it is a BIG DEAL!

These two ladies, Liz and Tracie, "birthed" this book and essentially asked me to be the godmother. Being a godmother comes with tremendous responsibility. In case anything should ever happen to Liz or Tracie, I would be tasked with taking responsibility for the proper care and future of this book. It's not something I take lightly and again I say, "It is a BIG DEAL!"

This book that they "birthed" is so much more than a book. It is years of experience, of trial and error, of hard work, sweat, and likely, tears. Most business people are not willing to share this "behind the scenes" look but prefer to keep it all to themselves. Not Liz and Tracie. They have been there, done that, got the t-shirt, taken the t-shirt off, and designed their own t-shirts. Now, they're letting you try on the t-shirt for yourselves.

Now, why should you believe what I have to say? Because I said so (Does that work if I'm not a mom?) Probably not. Listen, I understand what it's like to "birth" an idea. I have also been on my own journey of entrepreneurship including Speaking, Coaching, and Training. I have had the pleasure of watching many different businesses, from small to large, grow from startups into mature, exciting and long-standing businesses.

I've been there for the heartaches, the successes, the highs and the lows, AND have experienced several of those myself. Many of the challenges I have seen with these businesses are addressed right here in this book. How often have you said to yourself "I wish there was a handbook?" Guess what? There is and you have it in your hands right now.

The generosity and passion Liz and Tracie have for helping other businessmen and women overcome those barriers is apparent all throughout this book. Nothing is held back and no translation required. Hell, they even give you two different viewpoints and perspectives. Liz is the nurturer, the one who holds your hand while showing you how to "adjust" or "tweak" your message. Tracie just pushes you out of the nest, because she knows you'll fly but you're afraid. Both of them, however, really do care about each and every person they touch. I'm telling you from experience that you will not find two people more devoted to others' successes.

AND if you're reading this, then you're lucky AND smart. You've already made a wise choice to invest in yourself by "inviting" these two into your life, plus I think I'm pretty funny to read, so bonus! Mostly, my hope is that you use this book as a guideline or roadmap and "try on the t-shirt."

So suck it up, do the work and believe in yourself as much as Liz and Tracie believe in what is possible for you.

Lisa Demmi

Speaker, Coach, Author
Small Magic

What Is This Book About?

According to the Bureau of Labor Statistics, only half of all new businesses make it through 5 years and only one third make it to their 10th anniversary.

That number has not changed in the past twenty years.

Regardless of technology, economic conditions, access to education, availability of resources, and innumerable other factors, the fail rate for a new business is still the same, only half make it past five years.

We have a theory about this. First, let's just acknowledge some key points. We are not scientists and we have not conducted any meaningful statistical research. What we have is knowledge, skills, smarts, together with tried and true instincts that have kept each of us in business for over ten years. As Mastermind Facilitators, Business Coaches, Mentors, and Stewards of a business networking organization, we have gained what we feel is a reasonable amount of perspective. How you absorb and apply that perspective is up to you.

Back to our theory about why success rates for new businesses have not changed in the past twenty years. It's simple – human behavior. Sure, technology has exploded around us, methods of communication have linked the globe, and there are thousands of business tools in the palm of your hand (literally, in your smart phone), but people are still people. And people LOVE to make excuses for themselves.

How do we know this? First, we've both done it. We will both readily admit that our businesses went from ho-hum to growth machines when we started masterminding together and engaging in some serious mutual accountability. Success started where the excuses ended!

Suck It Up, Buttercup is all about sharing that perspective with you and highlighting the ten most common excuses we've found to be self-imposed barriers to success. Do you need to be a business owner to benefit from this book? Goodness no! While our focus is in the small business space, these excuses apply to professionals across all roles.

Whether you have a business, are considering launching a business, work in the corporate world, sacrifice your all in the military (Thank You), or are retired and wanting to get back in the business mindset, this book can help you get past your own limits to start making measurable progress.

There are two voices throughout this book. In each chapter you will hear from Liz and Tracie independently. Why? Although we agree on how to overcome these ten excuses, our approach is different. This dual approach is the foundational strength when we lead mastermind groups and coach our clients.

If you prefer a more diplomatic message you will likely resonate to Liz's sections. She believes that the difference in where you are and where you want to be is connected to how tolerant you are of your own excuses. Liz is all about creating awareness and then inspiring you to action so that you tackle the mindset that is holding you back, commit to a plan, and work with fierce accountability.

If you respond better to getting the sense knocked into you, then you will enjoy the segments written by Tracie, the Guru of Common Sense. Her intelligent guidance is no nonsense, to-the-point, take your lumps, pick yourself up, and get it done!

Together, Liz and Tracie share insights to help you recognize your own excuses and then provide practical steps to overcome them. Every chapter includes mastermind encouragements to get you started with action. If you want to maximize the benefits of this book, we invite you to visit https://kmanetwork.com/buttercup-workbook to download the official companion workbook. Now, are you ready to suck it up and achieve more success than ever?

Who We Are

Before we launch into how to break free from the top 10 excuses that keep business owners stuck, allow us to briefly introduce ourselves.

Liz M. Lopez

I absolutely love being a Success Coach and a Speaker. Working with business owners, consulting with corporate teams, getting in front of audiences, it's all exciting. It is a privilege to ignite audiences by showing them their own potential and creating a clear path to accomplishing their true objectives.

After graduating with a dual degree in Sociology and Economics, plus an award-winning 15-year corporate career, I launched my own company, Captivate Your Audience, in 2007. Since then, I've worked with thousands of Professionals, Business Owners, Entrepreneurs, and Corporate Groups seeking to elevate their brand, communicate their value, and engage their target market. Over the years, I've also become known as a LinkedIn expert.

In 2013, I was looking to aggressively grow my business. I had strategic plans, but kept losing myself working in the business rather than ON the business. In other words, I was doing the daily running of the business, I was working with clients, but I was slacking in working on the strategic planning and implementations needed to grow my business.

Meeting Tracie and starting our mastermind sessions was transformational. I grew my business double-digits that year and I knew we had something special with our mastermind and accountability discipline.

In 2014, when fellow business owners kept asking what Tracie and I were doing differently, we launched the Keystone Mastermind Alliance (or KMA for short) and started facilitating Mastermind Groups. In four years, KMA has expanded to include Business Brainstorming Events, Business Workshops, Badass Business Bootcamps, Business Coaching, and hundreds of members have joined our Business Networking division: The KMA Network.

These days, I work exclusively with about six executives a month through Captivate Your Audience to develop their brand and plot career growth. I work with select business owners on their growth strategies, including LinkedIn coaching. I also do a lot of speaking at conferences and professional events, which I love. As President of the Keystone Mastermind Alliance, I am constantly developing new programs to elevate success for our business community. One of my great passions is the time I dedicate to coaching business owners through KMA. Seeing other business owners achieve and exceed the results Tracie and I have experienced is incredibly rewarding.

Tracie Thompson

After attending business school, I decided I hated panty hose. The short story is, I became a Personal Fitness Trainer working in large gyms. I was a bit different from other trainers because I understood that my job wasn't just training. I was running my own business within someone else's business and I studied intently what worked and what did not work. I saw great ideas and witnessed massive failures. Over the years, I supported operations, ran payroll, and mentored other Personal Trainers who were either starting out or struggling to book clients.

When Liz and I met in 2013, I was still working within a large gym. I had been preparing to open my studio for years, and through our mastermind discussions, I went from planning to executing. When I opened 4Fitness Studio, I set moderate goals about the number of new clients I would book for the year. I shattered those goals six months early. I attribute that success to everything I learned while working within other business structures, and the resources and solutions provided by my Mastermind partners.

Here is what I know: big companies don't just have one person making decisions. They have an Executive Leadership team and a Board of Directors. Together they make healthy decisions for the growth of the company, bring new ideas to the table, and join forces to overcome challenges. KMA closes this gap for Business Owners and Entrepreneurs giving them an even playing field when it comes to sharing knowledge and being held accountable.

Today, I train private clients one-on-one in the studio, manage the 4Fitness business which has expanded to include Yoga and other disciplines, lead operations for KMA, and coach business clients. Every moment of my working day is either improving someone's health or improving someone's wealth.

Together, We Achieve More

When we launched KMA, we knew we were offering important resources to the business community, especially small business owners and entrepreneurs. We know that the skyrocketing growth we've experienced in our own businesses is because we haven't allowed excuses. We have held each other accountable.

We've made it a point to share everything we know and we approach our business community with an open invitation. We don't "hide the good stuff" or try to keep our strategies a secret. Instead, we continuously develop platforms for others to learn and create methods for keeping our clients and our members fiercely accountable for their own success.

A constant phrase when things get tough, is Suck It Up, Buttercup. The discipline of no-excuses keeps us focused, and allows us to create a mastermind movement that is giving hundreds of business owners the tools they need to grow exponentially. Through this book, we are sharing that discipline with you, so that you too can break your self-imposed barriers and start racking up serious wins in your business or corporate career.

Intro

If you "build it they will come." At some point you had an amazing idea for a business so you shared it with the people in your world and they also thought it was a great idea. You start discussing the pros and cons of opening a business and inevitably someone says it: "If you build it, they will come."

It's not that simple. If you read *What Is This Book About*, then you already know that 50% of new businesses fail by their fifth year in business. Here is another data point for you from the Bureau of Labor Statistics: of the ones remaining, only about 33% make it to ten years.

Everyone gets really excited about starting a business, yet often do not understand the level of long-term commitment needed. Here is a truth: as monumental of an effort as it can be to start a business, it is nothing compared to what is takes to maintain a business. Most people succeed in getting their business started, the key is to keep it going, preferably profitably, for the long run.

Liz

The biggest lie Hollywood has ever told is build-it-and-they-will-come. *Field of Dreams* was a good movie. I wasn't a big Kevin Costner fan at the time (I'm liking older Kevin much better) but I admit that the movie was heartwarming and entertaining. Still, it was just a movie! It falsely gave people the idea, especially new business owners, that all they had to do was hang up a shingle, get a business card, put together a cheap website, and BOOM people will just start buying their stuff left and right...cars will be lining up across state lines...money will roll in. Right? Wrong!

It doesn't work that way.

People will not just come to your business whether it's a virtual business or brick and mortar establishment. This is evidenced by the very narrow long-term success rate of new businesses. There are tons of reasons why businesses fail. Poor capitalization, bad location, product nobody wanted, lack of marketing know-how, poor customer service, and so many more.

Wanna know a secret? Quality of product is not necessarily a reason for failure. Think about it. I bet you can think of several fast food joints that don't have the most delicious food on the planet and still they thrive. Similarly, you can probably think of at least one restaurant that had great food and yet it went under. Why do I mention this? Because using grandma's secret recipe to make the best meatballs in the world is not a guarantee for success.

Do you remember Blockbuster? Montgomery Ward? Sports Authority? How about the thousands of restaurants per year that go out of business within months of opening because they did not know how to attract their clientele? Maybe they had the best food in town, but sadly they went broke because not enough people knew that. The thought that "if you build it they will come" depletes new business owner's life savings every day.

Tracie and I have both been in business over 10 years. That tenure didn't happen by building our businesses and standing aside waiting for clients to magically appear. The truth is that you need to build your business every day. It. Never. Stops. Sure, after a while you perfect your systems, you develop a reputation, and it can get easier, however, you never really stop. If you want to thrive, you must constantly evolve to grow.

When you are a business owner, it really takes a lot more than just being good at one thing. Yes, you need to have a central talent that is at the bottom line of your product or your service. Still, there is more. You must be a good marketer, a good salesperson, a good customer experience manager, a good bookkeeper, a good inventory manager, a good negotiator, and the list goes on and on. Independent entrepreneurs and small business owners wear a lot of hats! You need to be prepared to do all those tasks or supervise those tasks when you assign or outsource them to others.

You can outsource lots of these functions to people who are experts in those arenas, but of course that is going to cost you money. So, you need to have those funds as part of your startup capital or have some really co-operative friends and relatives. Learn what you can and maybe engage in mutually beneficial trade with people in your local business network. Keep in mind that you need to know enough to make sure that the work others are doing for you aligns to your brand, and that it's quality work done in an effective and efficient manner. A former boss and dear friend, Lori, taught me that you must inspect what you expect!

The point is, you can't just put together a business and think that people are just going to come find you, love you, and give you all their money. That's pretty much a business fairy tale and it's the exception to the rule. The norm involves having a solid business plan, marketing plan, developing a clear message, reaching your target audience in a compelling manner, blowing their socks off with your product or service, delivering an outstanding customer experience, following up with effective customer loyalty strategies, and knowing your exit plan.

It's not magic, but it's not a mystery either. It is absolutely possible to launch a thriving business, it just takes more than wishful thinking. If you can wrap your head around the ongoing investment of energy, skill, and time that is takes to manage all the key aspects of your business, then your chances of beating the odds get a lot better.

You will see me say over and over again, it starts with mindset. You have to know that it will be an ongoing commitment. But here is the thing, if you have picked the right business for yourself, this will feel exciting, not overwhelming. Okay, sometimes it will feel overwhelming, but if you are following your passion, then it will be worth it. There is something very powerful about knowing you are investing in your own dream, whether it's a stellar corporate career or building a thriving business.

Remember, lots of people open businesses. Our purpose is to guide you in sustaining a business. When it comes to launching a business you need to ask yourself, am I willing to build it every day?

Tracie

The Field of Dreams mentality says, "I have a great business, a great business model, people will buy my product or service." No matter what your business structure looks like: direct sales, digital services, or running a brick and mortar, a truly needed service or product does not ensure that people will flock to your business.

Let me explain. You decide to have a party next Friday. Everyone loves a party. You planned for it. You picked the date. You picked the time. You planned a menu. You even have a theme (maybe a luau party?). You shopped for food and drinks. You set up the party area, decorated, cooked, and put the food out. You planned your outfit, showered, and got dressed. It's going to be the best party ever!

Now here it is Friday 8 pm, party time and you are all alone. Why? Because, you made a critical mistake! You didn't tell anyone about your party. You didn't tell them when it was, where it was, or how great it was going to be. You didn't invite anyone to your party! How were they supposed to know to show up? People can't read your mind.

Your business is just like this example. You actually have to invite people to your business. In fact, it is essential that you invite them to do business with you. You must tell people who you are, and what you and your business are all about. What is your product or service? What makes it so special? How do they buy it? Where do they buy it? When can they buy it? How much does it cost? How does it all a work?

You can't just have a party and never tell anybody about it. You can't just have a business and not tell everyone about it. Opening a business and hoping people find you by accident because you have something amazing is not a plan, it's not effective. You must invite people to your business.

Make it easy for people to find you or contact you. There are many ways of doing this and we could write a whole other book on marketing strategies (and maybe we will), but here are some easy examples: List your business with Google & Apple maps. Make sure all your social media profiles include a way to contact you including address, email, phone number, and website.

In today's world of cell phone usage make sure that your information is clickable, when your phone number is clicked on, it should dial, when your email address is clicked it should open an email, and make sure that your website is a link. No one does business with a company or person they can't easily find and contact. Customers will not hunt you down. It's not their job to hunt you down, it is your job to make it easy for them to do business with you.

I know what you're thinking. I don't want my phone number out there for everyone to see. Well, then get a separate number for your business or get over it. Do you want privacy or do you want customers? Let's be real, phone numbers and addresses are not really secrets and with a little effort most can be found. If you are willing to put it on your business card it shouldn't be a big deal to put it on Facebook or Google. Now if you run a business from your home, you don't want your home address out there, I get that, you don't have to share your private address. Just make sure that your business phone number and email are highly visible.

Many good business ideas fail due to marketing or lack of marketing. Marketing is a whole division of business because being there or being open is not enough to make a business succeed. You need to be visible, searchable, accessible, and an excellent, consistent inviter.

Liz mentioned that you need to build your business every day and I am sure that some of you will read that and think "no, once I get everything going it will take care of itself." I want to put a stop to that thinking right here.

Have you heard of Coca-Cola? Of course, you have! Do you think it is safe to say that just about everyone in the United States is familiar with Coca-Cola? It's even reasonable to say that most people across the world are familiar with Coca-Cola. Okay, we have established just about everyone has heard of Coca-Cola, is familiar with it, and that's why you never see television ads for Coca-Cola. Right?

Hold on, that's not true. They are always advertising on TV, billboards, radio, magazines, and in movie theatres. They even come up with new campaigns like putting names on the cans so you can share a Coke with a friend. They sponsor major events like NASCAR Races, Olympic Games, and Super Bowls.

Coca-Cola spends $565 million on advertising in the U.S., according to Ad Age Datacenter. The company reported spending $3.3 billion on advertising globally in 2013.

Coca-Cola, who is an established recognized brand that has been successful in lasting 125 years, continues to brand, market, and advertise their business to the tune of $3.3 billion. I urge you to really think about and digest that last sentence. If a company like Coca-Cola continues to build its business every day, why do you think your small business doesn't need to?

Summary

We love being business owners and it's never our intention to discourage anyone from an entrepreneurial path. On the contrary, we applaud everyone who has the courage to launch their own business. We want more business owners to succeed. A consistent 50% fail rate in 5 years is ridiculous! We can do better!

Every chapter in this book is meant to help you do better and beat the odds. It all starts with being realistic and getting grounded by what it means to sustain and grow a business. Pace yourself. We see so many business owners killing themselves to meet self-imposed launch deadlines that by the time they open, they are already burned out.

Starting a business is exciting and it can be so much fun. Just make sure that you are not just planning a launch. When we work with start-ups, our objective is to be realistically encouraging. Our guidance to you is the same as it is to our Mastermind clients: Have a comprehensive and achievable plan for creating success every single day after opening. Dreaming big is great Buttercup, but it's not fun when dreams crash and burn because you didn't take the right actions to sustain those bold dreams.

Chapter One: Mastermind Encouragement

Don't just hope to make it, PLAN to succeed. Naturally, your plans will evolve over time. However, starting with a picture of where you want to be in the long run grounds you and gives you a path to follow.

1. Create a 1, 5 and 10 year plan for your business. This can be a detailed multipage document or quick outlines.
2. Be sure to include your exit plan. How you build a

business that you intend to sell differs from a business you will leave to your kids or close when you retire. Start with the end in mind.

3. Take your Year 1 plan and break it down into a 12-Month Action Plan. Carefully prioritize and be aware of seasonal changes in your industry or local area.

4. Take Action. Get an accountability partner or a business coach and make sure you are systematically working your plan. It's easy to get bogged down in the day-to-day.

5. Be aware. Keep your eye on short-term AND long-term business needs.

Intro

When creating a business, it's smart to think about the reach of your particular business. How many people could use your product or service? It is a common thought that a business with a wide reach is better than a business with a narrow market. If only ten people in the whole world will buy what you are selling, then you are likely not going to last long. That is, unless you sell ten items that cost billions each, then congrats on that unique business model!

Many entrepreneurs and sales professionals brag about getting involved with companies that sell products that "everyone" can use. Here is the skinny, even if all seven billion plus people on this planet can use your product or service, it does not follow that everyone will buy it.

That is why there is more than one brand for just about everything available for sale around the world. Think about it, just about everything sold comes in a variety of colors. Consumers have different tastes, brand allegiances, service expectations, price demands, etc. Failing to tune into the nuances of your target market can cause you to fail, even with a product you are convinced you can sell to everyone.

Liz

I have been a business owner for 10 years and I do a

lot of business networking in local and national groups. In fact, Tracie and I own and operate a local networking organization with hundreds of members (www.kmanetwork.com). Believe me when I tell you that there is a stigma attached to people who come in to networking meetings and gleefully announce that they can sell to anybody.

This is especially true when asked who makes a good referral for their business. Saying that you can sell to everybody and anybody does not make you relatable to a greater target market. On the contrary, it tells your audience that you don't know how to communicate who is in your target market.

Let me give you some examples of this. You have a skin care lotion and your thought process is "I can sell this product to anybody with skin, because anybody with skin could use the lotion." It seems intuitive, but in reality that train of thought is flawed. Consider this, everyone in the world could choose to drink a Coke or a Pepsi, but some are going to drink a Coke and some a Pepsi and they are not going to go across those brand lines. Loyalty is involved there.

People have individual tastes, choices, preferences, and different types of budgets. Just because someone could apply the lotion to their skin doesn't mean that they want your specific lotion and even if they want it, that doesn't mean they can afford it. Furthermore, even when they want it and can afford it, they may not want to buy it from you.

Yes, personality sways a lot of buying decisions. When I am in a grocery store, I am selective about choosing a check-out line. I intentionally line up where the cashier seems chipper and quick. It doesn't matter if it's the shortest line, I want the best check out experience possible. I'm still buying everything in my cart, so I am picky about who I buy it from. Think about it, you don't just go to any hairstylist, doctor, dentist, accountant, etc. Typically, you ask for recommendations, do some research and pick the provider you liked the best. In general, its human nature to not want to give money to people we don't like.

Is it becoming clear that there is no such thing as "anybody will buy my service?" The better you get at understanding who is willing and able to buy your product and services the better you are going to do. Let's talk a bit more about the concept of *willing and able*.

In my late twenties, I worked in the Credit Decisioning department for a large credit card company. I had to review applications from individuals applying for very high credit limits and determine whether that person was likely to pay back however much they spent on their credit card. My teammates and I would look at the applicant's credit history, income, and their financial situation to get a sense of their ability and willingness to payback what they owed. A strong indicator was past behavior - have they demonstrated that when they borrowed money, they paid it back?

Ability and willingness are two factors that will

intersect whether it is for loans or a product you are selling. People must be willing to part with their money to purchase what you are selling. Not everyone goes to the movie theatre because some people don't feel like it's worth paying $11 to go see a movie. Back in the Napster days people would download "free" music because they weren't willing to spend their money buying music. What people are willing to open their wallet for varies from person to person. You need to get really good at knowing who is willing to open their wallet for what you are selling.

It's marketing at its most basic – identifying your target market. This is what connects everything and makes it all work. Do you know who is willing and able to spend money on what you offer? Does your marketing plan identify these people and do your marketing campaigns reach them? Are you using the right words and images with the right approach to appeal to that group of people that will most likely buy your product or service? And beyond that, is your sales system set up to get these potential buyers from interested to customers?

There is both an art and science to being successful in business. This "everybody, anybody, somebody" stuff doesn't work. Honestly, the "everybody" approach is a little lazy. You're not taking the time to truly understand the people who are going to be your best clients. You're going to put yourself through hard changes if you truly believe in "everybody, anybody" because you are going to be constantly disappointed. Every time you do a sales pitch or demonstration and people don't buy, you are going to be flabbergasted and dealing with rejection. Avoid the pain!

Change your mindset and do the work. You can do this! Let go of the fear that you are going to miss out on sales if you don't pitch to everyone. In fact, you will close more sales and make more money when you are directing your efforts towards a target market that is willing and able to buy your product. Would you try to sell snow shovels to homeowners in Florida?

I love an optimist, but you also have to be realistic in business. The idea that everyone can benefit from your product is naïve. Even if it's true, it doesn't follow that everyone is going to pay for your product or service. The more you understand about who is willing to part with their dollars for what you offer, the more successful you are likely to be. Spend the time and effort to clearly identify your target market segments and finding clients will never be your issue.

Tracie

"I can do business with anyone with skin, anyone with an air conditioner, anyone with a home". I am not sure why small business owners fear that by clearly defining their target market or niche market that they, by default, are saying they won't do business with other people.

It's just an absurd thought! No business does business with everyone and anyone. There is always an ideal client or an ideal market for your business. I think this "I can sell to anyone" routine is a lazy excuse to avoid figuring out who your ideal client really is. You're just hurting your success.

When you don't know who your client is, your marketing dollars are wasted trying to get everyone. Anytime we look at data there is always information that is considered a trend and some information that falls outside the trend, the outlier. There will always be outliers. As a business owner do you want to market to the segment of people most likely to do business with you or to the people who don't fit the trend but maybe, once in a while, may do business with you?

A perfect example is my fitness boutique. The basic niche or target market that responds best to my business model are women between the ages of 45 and 65. Does that mean that I don't train men? No! Of course, I train men. I have just found that the men that I train are typically the spouse or the brother or somehow related to a woman I already train. So, I wouldn't say I don't train men but when it comes to marketing, they are not my primary target market.

If I am spending marketing dollars, I don't want to go after men when I know that I mainly acquire male clients through my existing female clients. Instead, I want to target those female clients because they are the ones who respond best to my business model. I want to use my marketing dollars in the most effective way.

So, when you have these business owners who say "Well, anyone who needs to lose weight" or "Everyone has skin so I can sell my magic moisturizer to anybody". Really, can you? Anybody is the homeless guy on the corner. Is the homeless guy on the corner going to buy your magic moisturizer? Okay so that example is over the top, but who is "anyone"?

Here is a more realistic example. The fitness industry can, in theory, work with anyone who needs to lose weight. Statistically 45% of adults are not sufficiently active to achieve health benefits and Americans ages 40-59 have the highest obesity rate of any age group at 41.0 percent (according to the stateofobesity.org). If this is all true, then the fitness industry has a huge amount of clients, right?

Not really. The statistics are true and the fitness industry has a large amount of potential clients, POTENIAL. The key word is potential and here is why. Out of the 41% of obese 40-59 year olds some of them are happy that way, which means they have no need for a gym or trainer. Some of those people are not able to afford a gym or trainer. Some of those people do not make losing weight a priority in their life and put work or family first. Some of those potential clients are highly motivated to change their weight and health and will do it on their own. Some of the 40-59 year old people will want to improve their weight and health and will want assistance. These are the people who will join a gym or hire a trainer and have the time and finances to do so. Do you see how there is a specific type of person who is most likely to buy what you are selling?

If you're not sure who is most likely to buy your

product or service look at who is already buying from you. What do your clients have in common? How old are they? Are they male or female? Do they live in a particular city or neighborhood? This information is at the very surface level and easy to gather. At a deeper level, if you take the time, you will find out a lot of things about your customers that then allow you to advertise to them.

Here is an example. Through the years I learned that most, about 70% of my fitness clients, own a boat. Whether it was small, medium, or large. So, advertising in a marina might not be such a bad idea even though it seems like an odd place to advertise for a personal training studio. But it is a common denominator in my clients. When exploring innovative marketing avenues, look for those common threads in your base clientele. Because while you really can't sell your product to anyone, you CAN sell your product quicker faster and with less marketing expenses when you know exactly who your customer is.

Summary

Here is our bottom line. You can't sell to everyone. You could be selling air, and we'd still call bullshit (Tracie said that) on your universal approach. Want to sell more? Stop the madness (Liz said that), please stop burning time and money promoting your product or service to people who are never going to buy it.

Did you know that big multinational companies spend millions of dollars to narrow their target market to one person? Maybe it's a 34 year old soccer mom with at least

iving in a three bedroom home with one dog and
it least 30 hours per week. YES, they get that
ѕрессиच. You may not need to, but you have to do better than
"everybody."

Put in the work to identify the people who are able
and willing to buy what you are selling. If you don't have the
first clue about target market analysis, make it a point to
learn. We have seen clients completely transform their
business and income simply by narrowing their focus.

Chapter 2: Mastermind Encouragement

You can do this exercise for your total business inventory or
you can break it down by product or service.

1. Is your product or service best aligned to business
   clients or consumers?
2. Who typically buys what you sell? Men or Women?
3. What age group(s) buys what you sell?
4. Is there an income level trend among your buyers?
5. What are some lifestyle characteristics of your
   frequent or ideal buyers?
6. How do they typically buy from you? (Ex: Buy on the
   website, visit my store, contact me via email, etc.)
7. Use these insights when building your marketing plan,
   messaging, and campaigns so they will align with
   your ideal/primary client.

Intro

Clients are the life blood of a business. Acquiring new clients is a necessity like the heart is to your body. Businesses spend an arm and a leg on marketing and advertising to attract new clients and when it isn't going well you may find yourself wishing for a lobotomy. A business without enough paying clients will soon go out of business. It's scary when your pipeline is empty.

Today, there are more avenues than ever to reach clients. Multi-channel marketing and omni-marketing are prevalent terms signaling the multi-tiered approaches many companies use to reach their unique customer segments. Traditional marketing methods such as direct mail, print ads, television ads, and radio spots are still alive despite a strong migration to digital marketing. Today, it's common to see print ads driving traffic to websites and social network platforms.

Client acquisition can be sophisticated or it can be grassroots (or both). There are so many ways to reach clients and many of them are so affordable that if you are not reaching clients, there is something seriously wrong with your marketing and sales process. The good news is, it can be fixed.

Liz

I'm going to ask a pointed question and I want you to consider a true, unfiltered answer. When it comes to finding clients...are you really looking? Are you looking in the right places? Are you looking for the right clients? This statement of "I can't find clients" brings up so many questions! When Tracie and I are working with our Mastermind groups and coaching clients it requires digging a little deeper because often the real issue is mindset. If you believe there are no clients, well, you are shaping that reality. For those who know clients are out there but can't tap into a reliable pipeline, often the issue is that they are not looking in the right places. It's like someone going up a snowy mountain and saying I can't find seashells.

If you have a viable and well-vetted product or service, then it's highly probable that you can find a market for it. The key here is to be willing to market and sell your product and service where the buyers are...which may not be where you are right now.

Hawking your wares and getting zero-to-little response is frustrating. Still, you need to know that rejection in business is something you have no choice but to learn to take. Your heart and mind need to know that you are not going to close every sale or convert every prospect. If you open a store in a neighborhood, not everyone in that neighborhood is going to stop in your store. Coca-Cola keeps marketing because after decades of being in business, not everyone drinks Coke. There is no such thing as a consistent 100% close rate. It is never going to be perfect.

The good news is that over time you will understand your close rate. When I get a referral in my executive resume business from someone I have done business with, I have a 90% chance of booking that client. When I get a stranger who finds me on LinkedIn, that close rate goes down to 60%, which is still darn good. Still, I understand that different sources of potential clients come with differences in people's ability and willingness to buy my product or service.

What does this all mean in terms of finding clients? Well, first make sure you are doing the right things to attract someone to you and that you are attracting the right clients. Which means you must know who your client is. We have talked about this before and you just can't adopt this mindset of I can sell to "anybody, everybody, somebody." You really have to put in the time and effort to clearly define your target market. The clearer you are on those demographics and characteristics, the better you can target the people most likely to become clients.

Once you know who is most likely to buy your product or service, the next step is to identify how to reach them. Without getting too technical, you need to have an idea of where your potential clients spend their time and identify the right marketing channels to reach them where they are.

The "catch" so to speak is that "where they are" can be a virtual, not only a physical space. You can use radio to reach people in their cars or offices and direct mail is still a very effective way to reach people at home. There are many relevant traditional marketing strategies that can reach potential customers in their specific physical space. Yet, more and more companies and business owners are turning to digital marketing strategies that allow you to reach clients in their "virtual spaces" such as Facebook, LinkedIn, Twitter, YouTube, Instagram, etc.

Just as there is really no guaranteed success in "build it and they will come", similarly there is no such guaranteed success with "post it and they will buy". There needs to be strategy and intelligence behind your digital marketing or you are just going to waste words and images in a vast and crowded cyberspace.

You need to determine if you are throwing your net into the right body of water. That is usually where we find the issue when working with our clients. They are using the wrong kind of net in a pond that doesn't have the fish they want or that are going to eat the bait they are offering. This doesn't mean that we are reducing your clients to fish or your product to bait. It's simply meant to illustrate that without putting yourself in front of your target market, even the most beautifully crafted words, images, video, infographics, etc. won't help you.

Do the work. Market analysis can be done using very sophisticated methods and can also be just as effective using grassroots method. Ask former clients questions, read industry news, or talk to direct and indirect competitors and find out what is working for them. Test different channels and campaigns. Marketing is all about testing, measuring, and adjusting until you find the message and channel that gets you the best return on your investment.

I get it. Someone became a millionaire selling a Pet Rock and we would all like to think we have the next million-dollar idea. Closely analyze your issue. Are you not reaching clients? Or are you reaching them and not closing them. Those are two distinct issues. The first speaks to a marketing issue. The second could be a sales issue or it could indicate that you have a product or service that is simply not fitting a need or a desire in the population you are reaching.

Be brutally honest with yourself. Living in a state of denial is not going to grow your business and it won't put money in your pocket. Be open and prepared to hear that your business may need to change, then take proactive action. There are millions of people out there shopping every day. With the right product, at the right price, offered to the right people, in the right channel you can give the Pet Rock guy a run for his money.

Tracie

There are no clients out there, the economy is bad, no one is buying. No, no, no! I'm sorry sweetheart, what you meant to say is that no one is buying from YOU! Because, trust me, if there were no clients out there and no one was buying anything, it would be all over the news. Companies everywhere would be closing their doors. Lexus, Mercedes, and Amazon would be going out of business. The question is, why are you not finding any clients? Or even better, why are clients not finding you?

Even in a bad market, like when the housing market crashed, houses were still selling just not as quickly as they did in a high market. It was a downturn not the end of home sales. When real estate agents in that time period said, "I can't find clients", they just weren't marketing to the clients who were willing to buy in that market. This is true of any business. If you feel like there are no clients out there, then you need to look at your product or service. Is it valuable and are you marketing it correctly? Are you trying to reach the market who wants your product or service?

Here is a great example: I don't do bodybuilding, I don't have an interest in training body builders and it's not where my knowledge base sits in the fitness world (Not that there is anything wrong with bodybuilding, it's just not my niche). If you've seen photos of me, then you know that I am a curvy personal trainer. I am not likely to attract bodybuilders as clients. If all my marketing was aimed at body builders, I would feel like there were no clients out there.

My studio doesn't have the equipment needed for bodybuilding, so bodybuilders wouldn't be interested in training there. My website says nothing about bodybuilders, but if I started putting ads out there that said, "Are you getting ready for your next body building competition, contact me" of course there would be no clients! By marketing a service to a population that doesn't fit my business model, I am wasting advertising dollars, wasting time, wasting energy, setting myself up for disappointment, and putting the longevity of my business at risk.

Let's get back to your world. Why are there no clients? Is your marketing in line with the population that uses your product or service? Either there is a misalignment or you are not looking. Is it that you are not looking? You might be thinking "of course I'm looking", but when we dig deep within our individual mastermind sessions, the truth we uncover is startling. Business owners think they are looking for clients, but really, they are not.

Sometimes people tell me there are no clients out there and I ask,

"What have you tried?"

"Oh, I post on Facebook"

"How often?"

"I'm not sure, maybe once a week, you know when I get a chance"

"Are you posting on a personal page or business page?"

"Mostly my personal, I don't really understand how my

business page works"

"So, do your posts get a lot of likes?"

"Sometimes, mainly friends and family. They are really supportive"

Just to be clear, occasional posts that get likes by your parents and Aunt Mildred is NOT SOCIAL MEDIA MARKETING and the example above does not qualify as "I've been looking for clients." Even with a well-planned social media marketing campaign, you may not drive clients through your front door on a regular basis. A haphazard approach or just winging it, is a great way to be in that 50% of failed businesses.

So, there might be no clients because you aren't really looking and you may need to try a better marketing strategy. Whether that's a Facebook ad or a landing page that you're driving prospects to, maybe calling up prior clients to touch base, calling current clients and asking for referrals. How about networking regularly?

A business owner told me they couldn't find clients. When I asked if they do any networking and they said "NO." Why not? Why would you not want to network and let other business owners know about your business so when they are in contact with consumers that say, "Do you know a "fill in the blank" they can say "Yeah, I do I know a great person who does that. May I give you a referral?" That's a free lead, that's a potential client you didn't have to go out and directly get, it is sent to you.

There are many ways to get clients, so when you feel like you can't find them you need to reevaluate. Are you really looking for them? How are you looking for them? And is everything lined up to attract them?

You need to make sure that you have a clear message inviting your target markets or ideal clients to do business with you. Make sure that your message is attractive and understandable to your target market. Be consistent with your marketing, networking, and posting on social media, especially when it is working.

Don't slow down when you're busy, keep pushing forward, and build on the momentum you have created. Don't let the fear of getting too busy hold you back. Too busy is the best problem your business could ever have. The solution is simple, outsource tasks that someone else can handle and or hire staff to do the work.

Summary

If you truly, honestly, really believe that there are "no clients out there", then it's time to pack it in, Buttercup. I mean, would you try to feed yourself everyday by fishing in a pond that you were convinced didn't have any fish? If you don't think there are clients out there, then why bother looking?

Maybe you are hoping to be convinced? By whom? By what? Are you randomly promoting your business with a d see attitude? Do you think this busload of clients will suddenly pull up and prove to you that there are clients in the universe?

If that's your approach and you are married to it, well, good luck (and you are going to need lots of it). Yes, success does sometimes present itself to the most unprepared and unlikely business owners, but that is the exception. Business owners who make it, make it deliberately. They make it because they believe there are buyers out there and they build a reasonable and achievable plan to find, engage, and retain clients.

If you believe there are clients, but are not finding them or not enough to sustain your business long term, then it's time to evaluate what you are selling, how you are selling it, who are you selling it to, and where you are trying to sell.

If you had a steady stream of clients but suddenly your pipeline is dry, you don't have time to panic, to feel sorry for yourself, or to complain. Any business can get into a rut. Maybe you were so busy with clients that you neglected your marketing. Learn from that and focus on aligning your product/service to your target clients.

Chapter 3: Mastermind Encouragement

Follow these steps to find and create paths to new clients.

1. Consider the past 12 months and analyze where your clients came from.

2. How did past clients find you? Are your marketing efforts aligned to this?
3. Have you asked for referrals?
4. Redirect marketing dollars and efforts into channels that have been productive and track results.
5. Consider testing new channels, just make sure to carefully track results so you know what worked and what didn't.

Intro

"I don't like sales." We wish we had a dollar for every time we have heard someone say, "I don't like sales" or "I'm just not a salesperson." We could easily have taken that money and used it to buy our own island. This is an all too common statement among entrepreneurs and it's usually said with a certain pride. We even hear business owners saying that they don't sell, they just educate. Guess what? Educating your client market is a sales technique. So is "sharing" and "helping!"

There is this twisted idea that sales are a bad thing. Somehow the idea of selling is seen as underhanded or sleazy. After all that honorable and noble work that Zig Ziglar did to legitimize the sales profession, some people still think "sales" is a dirty word and proclaim, "I don't like sales" like some badge of honor.

What's worse, is that they don't see that there is a huge issue with their statement. They don't understand how self-defeating it can be and furthermore how such an attitude can keep them from learning a skill that is critical to the survival of their business.

Good Ol' Merriam-Webster defines the act of selling as "the transfer of ownership of and title to property from one person to another for a price." Unless you intend to donate or give away your product or service, this is exactly what you are trying to do. The sooner you make peace with that and get good at it, the better.

Liz

Oh Buttercup, it really doesn't matter what product or service your company is promoting, if you are a single entrepreneur doing it on your own, a small business owner with a team, or even if you're part of a large corporation - it's always about sales. You might be selling a product, a service, a relationship, or your own professional brand. Tracie usually takes the hardline, but there is one statement that will get my blood boiling. "I just want to help people."

No. You. Don't.

If you just want to help people then don't launch a business, go do volunteer work! I hear all the time from struggling business owners "It's not about the money, I just want to help people." Sigh, it hurts my heart because it's such a loaded statement. It often speaks to a poor relationship with money and an underlying guilt about making money, especially if your product or service serves a basic life need.

Let's be very clear, it doesn't matter if your product was the very nectar of life, you have a right to make a living. You can't call your electric company and tell them that you need to skip this month's payment because you were too busy helping people and didn't generate any sales. Do that for a couple of months in a row and you will be helping people in the dark.

It is absolutely okay for you to make money. In fact, it is absolutely okay for you to make a LOT of money. If you are going to be a business owner, be sure your heart and mind are communicating and that they agree in abundance. It breaks my heart to see women and men struggle to value themselves. They stutter when they need to talk about price and they give out discounts left and right without even being asked. Stop it. You have every right to make money, okay? Can we agree on that?

The thing is, that to make money you are going to have to sell. Often when people think about sales they conjure images of the infamously slick and greasy used car salesman. It's time to let go of that prejudice. Besides, we all engage in sales every day without even realizing it.

Let me take the extreme version of this and let's talk about corporate professionals. You work in a job and you have nothing to do with the sales department. Perhaps you work in accounting, billing, the warehouse, manufacturing, etc. and you think you don't have anything to do with sales. This is not quite correct.

You see, at the very least you are selling your own performance. Every single day you must prove that you have value because if you don't have value, if you're not engaging with your team, if you're not producing what needs to be produced, then your job might be in jeopardy. Think about performance reviews, there is some salesmanship involved in making sure your boss knows all the value you added throughout the year. You are selling your leadership team on the premise that you deserve a great score, and ideally, a generous raise.

So now let's move to the flip side of that. Maybe you're a business owner with a group of employees, a team, or you're a solo entrepreneur, either way, it is necessary for you to be able to sell the value of what you are delivering to your customers and your clients. Whether you're a Plumber, Dentist, Nutritionist, Mechanic, etc., you are in sales. You must have some kind of engagement with gatekeepers and decision makers to get them to like and trust you enough to even consider buying from you.

Furthermore, you are not just selling a doodad or service but an amazing experience. Two hairstylists can cut hair the same way, but if one offered a wonderful experience and you really enjoyed the time and the other was rushed or you felt mistreated, aren't you are going to go to the hairstylist that treated you nicely and made you feel better? That is all part of how you are selling yourself and your value.

Everything from your likeability, to your communications skills, to your follow-up matters. Your entire sales cycle encompasses introducing yourself and making yourself known to others to eventually get to the point where you actually close the sale and exchange goods and services for money. And then, there is how you follow up and create customer loyalty. It's all sales!

You are not just a plumber, you are a plumber who sells plumbing services. You are not just a stylist, you are a stylist who sells great styles that inspire confidence. You are not just a bookkeeper, you are a skilled individual that makes your clients feel that their money is accurately accounted for. Regardless of your industry or trade, if you are an entrepreneur, business owner, or even a corporate professional – you are in sales. And that really is okay.

Last year I bought a car at CarMax. It was my best car buying experience ever. So even the old (and very unfair) stigma of the used car salesman needs to go out the window. Sales people are not all self-interested sleaze balls. When Tracie and I teach sales seminars or we coach clients in building an effective sales process, changing that mindset is always the first step.

Personally, I suggest that you conduct yourself with integrity, embrace sales, and learn what it takes to get really good at sales. You can't escape sales! If you can't become skilled in "the transfer of ownership of and title to property from one person to another for a price", then you are going to need to get really good at selling yourself in a job interview when your business becomes another sad statistic. I know that feels harsh, but it's true. If you want to beat the odds, you must become comfortable with sales.

Tracie

Okay, you don't like sales. Do you like money? Do

you like new customers? Unfortunately, sales, although it is a dirty word to many people, is part of doing business. You don't have to like it, you must learn how to do it. And you absolutely need to do it. If you really don't like sales maybe you should hire someone to do it for you because sales are an integral part of doing business. When you get down to it, selling shouldn't feel uncomfortable if what you are offering customers is a valuable product or service that they want.

Why do we insist on viewing sales as such a dirty, nasty thing? You don't have to be what we think of as the "used car salesman." You are not trying to sell someone something they don't want or need. If you know who your target market is, chances are you are marketing to someone who is looking for your product or service. I hear it all the time in a whiny voice "I don't like sales". "I don't like having to ask people for money". Then you shouldn't own a business.

Money and sales are always going to be a part of business. How many clients walk away because you didn't ask for the money or you didn't even ask for the sale? If you are really that uncomfortable with sales, get yourself some sales training. Whether you do that with us or another coach, get some training. It will make sales so much more comfortable and effective.

Here's the great news: you get to choose how you do sales. Me personally, I hate the high-pressure sales tactic. "I need you to make up your mind right now. Why would you not buy my product or service I told you how great it is you said you need it and yet you're still waiting". I'm not a fan of right now or let me call my manager to explain it better or help you decide. I don't like that done to me, so I would never do that to a potential client.

I get to choose how I approach selling my services. I may have a very strong voice on a lot of things and I can be very no nonsense, but when it comes to selling to a potential customer I tend to be on the softer side of sales. I present the value of my service. I explain it and I take every opportunity to answer questions as best and as fully as is possible. Then I tell potential clients "It is up to you how we proceed, these are the options". It makes sales not "salesy."

Let me emphasize that. Sales doesn't have to be "salesy." Explain the value, position your offers (typically A, B, & C) and let them tell you how they'd like to proceed. When someone says, they need time to think about it, I let them. I'm not going to call in a heavy weight to close the deal. I am not going to pressure them with "What is your problem? What do you have to think about? Why would you want to wait?" Let them wait.

Be proactive, ask "Is it okay if I follow up with you next week? Can I call you in a couple of days to see what you're thinking?" Those are options for you. This way you don't feel like your nagging them. Or "I would love to follow up with you, what is the best way to contact you, email or a phone call?" There are so many ways to do sales that are not salesy and sleazy. Educate yourself on the diverse ways to sell. If you're not sure, talk with someone who you like the way they sell. Take a class or an online webinar, get a coach. There are so many options, use one and get selling.

Summary

"Sales" is not a dirty word and your sales practices never have to feel uncomfortable or underhanded. You get to define your sales process including presenting your value, inviting sales, and conducting your follow-up. You control every aspect of the sales dynamic for your business and you have the ability to make it AMAZING.

If you do not have a defined sales process for your business. It's time to develop one. When you know the touch points your business needs to convert a prospect into a client, you can plan every stage and make sure your process feels natural and honest. Maybe your sales process is low key, maybe it's a bit more assertive – there are many sales strategies and techniques. Your job is to stop denying you are in sales, and embrace a sales approach that best matches your core values and your target market's expectations.

Develop your sales process and then practice, practice, practice. Avoid winging it or making it up as you go along. Success in sales often rests in being able to clearly communicate value in a compelling manner. Use the questions below to draft a simple sales process then video yourself talking through it. Analyze where you stumble and fix it!

ıles doesn't come naturally to everyone. That's why it's important to prepare, have a plan, and practice, practice, practice!

1. What do you say when someone asks about your product or service?
2. List the features and benefits for all of your products and services.
3. Write out your process for discussing prices with interested buyers.
4. How do you ask for the sale? Be specific.
5. Rehearse your sales presentation and record yourself on audio and video. Do you sound and look confident? Do you falter at any point? Keep practicing!
6. What is your method for following up with those who say "not right now"? If you don't have one, create one.
7. What is your method for following up with former clients? If you don't have one, create one.

Intro

"I don't like to brag." Well, that's okay because no one wants to listen to someone talk about themselves all the time. It is easy to agree that no one likes to listen to someone bragging about themselves or their business. Can we also agree that not being able to speak comfortably about yourself and your business may be hindering your success?

No one is telling you to prance around putting on airs or to go "Kardashian" on social networks. This chapter is about the difference between bragging and speaking with confidence. In our networking organization, mastermind groups, and private coaching sessions, we have seen business owners literally shrink into themselves when asked about their products or services. Our intention is for you to be able to clearly discuss your value without feeling guilty or nervous that you might be bragging.

Liz

The American Marketing Association defines marketing as, "the activity, set of institutions, and processes for creating, communicating, delivering, and exchanging offerings that have value for customers, clients, partners, and society at large". Bragging, on the other hand, is defined as "excessively proud and boastful talk about one's achievements or possessions".

Marketing your product or service involves the communication of value. Bragging is boasting and gloating. There are not the same! There isn't anything noble about diminishing yourself. In fact, Maryann Williamson wrote a powerful poem about that, which many recall being read by Nelson Mandela. You know, the one that says:

We ask ourselves
Who am I to be brilliant, gorgeous, talented, fabulous?
Actually, who are you not to be?

You have every right to confidently speak about the best of yourself as well to describe your products and services in a positive light. Got it? Are we good here?

Okay, just in case you are still feeling conflicted about this, I will expand. How you present and explain your products and services needs to align with your personality. If you are a quiet, reserved person, then a blustery, in-your-face approach is going to make you uncomfortable and most likely fail. Does that mean you can't sell? No, of course not. There are a lot of ways to powerfully position your products and services without having to feel like a jackass.

The key here is to develop a sense of comfort and confidence about the VALUE of your products of services. You never, ever have to brag or boast. You just need to tell an honest story to the right audience using the ideal communication channel(s) for your target market.

You can use success stories, before and after pictures, customer testimonials, customer ratings, and lots of other tools that allow your product or service to prove itself. Think about it. Have your clients benefited from what you offer? Did you give them a fair price and quality service? If the answer is yes, then communicating that to others is not bragging, its' inviting them to also acquire that value.

Tracie and I have worked with clients with deep seated and even faith-based commitment to humility. These business owners were (still are) incredibly talented and offered valuable products or service. Yet, they were held back by a fear of appearing to be bragging. When we coached them through articulating their value in a factual, calm manner, they blossomed and their businesses got busier.

Here is my message to you Buttercup, you have permission to speak truthfully about the value you offer. You can discuss past achievements, share success stories, and even show some of your work – as long as you are doing it to impart value to others, rather than fishing for compliments.

If you don't tell your story, then who will? You are both the custodian and the messenger of your value proposition. Remember, the "build it and they will come" chapter? They won't! You must invite clients into your world, and to do that, you need to put out a compelling call-to-action. So, practice. Practice talking about your business. Practice in the mirror or on video. Watch yourself. Do you look confident? Is there a place where you stumble? Take a deep breath adjust your message, and practice it until you can deliver it with confidence.

This is your business, your dream, your income, your brand. If you don't sell it, who will? Sure, you might get to the point where you have a sales force doing all that for you, but you will have to train them. If you cannot confidently impact the value of your goods to your team, they won't be successful. You are not just imparting technical information, you also have to transfer your deep belief in the value of what you offer to the world.

Most often than not, the only real limitation a business owner has is their own fears. Please do not let fear or doubt hold you back. Avoid falling into the trap of being more comfortable with being broke than with being eloquent. Challenge yourself, push yourself out of your comfort zone, and find the right words to tell the world how awesome YOU and your products/services are.

Tracie

No one wants to brag. Nobody wants to be that person, you know that person who all they talk about is themselves in all their glory and greatness. No one wants to be self-centered or conceited, all that and a bag of chips. Okay, clearly some people do want to be that, but if you are not one of them, then don't be.

But for fudge sake, if you are not willing to talk about

your business, how great it is, the individuality of your business, and all things wonderful that your business brings to the world, then who the hell will? No one. No one will sing your praises because they won't know how great your business really is because you couldn't get over your personal image issues and let them in on the secret.

Ok, I lied. A few people will sing your praises like your mom, sister, best friend and a few customers who truly enjoyed their experience with your product or service. Then when potential customer, Judy, comes in and says: "Mary told me about you and she loved your business", you make that awkward face, giggle or say something lame and Judy is gone.

Don't lose your Judys! You need to get over it, you shouldn't be embarrassed that you work hard on and in your business and you gave Mary a product or service that she wanted. Awkward behavior makes it seem like you are unsure, not confident. What you should say is "I am happy that Mary had a great experience and shared it with you" or just a genuine thank you. Accept the compliment graciously and move on with business.

Here is the other problem with the scenario, Mary is only talking about what she loved about your business. What she talked about convinced Judy to come in, but Sara wasn't interested in what Mary was talking about. Since you are not putting out a more comprehensive message, Sara didn't know about your other services and never did business with you.

It is your job to express to your customers and prospects the many benefits of your business or service. This can be done in person, email, through social media, on your website or countless other channels. Highlighting aspects of your business is not bragging, it's educating. If your product is "Made in America" you should let people know because it matters to them. Is your product homemade by you? Tell your target market! If you offer a service that other people in your industry don't, people need to know, so they can make an informed decision. If you are a leader in your industry don't keep it a secret. These types of things add value to you and your brand.

Word of caution. Stay away from things like" "I make the best chocolate". Really? The best? According to whom? Now you're bragging. What you can do is educate potential clients on what makes your chocolate so good, such as the percentage of cocoa, the fact that its hand blended, etc., whatever applies. Another thing to be careful of is saying "Award winning" or "#1 Choice". Use these only if you actually have an award from somewhere credible and that it's recent, not some award from 10 years ago.

Still worried about bragging? Let's put some context around the idea of bragging about our business. It is not bragging to highlight the features of my business to someone who is genuinely interested in my service. Let's say a potential client books a consult. They actually expect me to tell them all about my business. That's not bragging, that's basic communication for my business.

Bragging would be meeting someone at a party and they say "What do you do?" and I proceed to ramble on and on about my highly successful personal training studio and everything that makes it great and unique until they see someone they just have to catch up with. Do you know what the difference is? Interest. Am I talking about my business because there is interest or because I want to? Don't let the fear of bragging keep you from talking about your business, skills, and achievements with interested people at appropriate times.

No one is or should be more qualified to talk about all the many details that set your business apart from all the others. Share information honestly and from a place of integrity. It is your job to overcome the fear of bragging and do your business the justice it deserves, including being spoken about with love and pride. Your customers and prospects will see your passion and you will see your business grow.

Summary

There is incredible beauty in a humble heart. But when that desire to be humble becomes paralyzing in your business, you may need re-set your balance.

You serve no one, by failing to stand tall for yourself. Instead, you likely cheat yourself, your employees, your family, and your clients when you fail to present your value with confidence.

Sure, clients may rave about you, friends may refer everyone they know, but in the end, if you cannot clearly convey the value of your products or services, your business will likely be at risk. If you struggle to deliver 30 second introductions, sales presentations, proposals, quotes, or flub answering questions about your prices, then you need to pause and figure out why.

The idea of needing to be humble may be real or it may be a convenient cover-up for a more deep-seated fear. Maybe you are afraid of speaking in front of people, maybe you hate rejection, maybe you are not sure what to do. All of these symptoms have a cure, they require action. You will need to step outside your comfort zone and embrace the idea that sharing your value proposition is your job. You launched the business, this is "your baby". You need to speak up about it.

Chapter 5: Mastermind Encouragement

Conveying value is sharing truth, not bragging. It helps to remember why you chose this path.

1. Why did you start your business?
2. What drives you to get up every morning?
3. What do your products or services do for your clients?
4. What do your competitors charge for similar products or services?
5. If you are shy to the point of not being able to speak in public, consider joining Toastmasters, find a mastermind group, find a coaching program, or even

get involved in community theatre.
6. Practice speaking confidently about your business. Video yourself and examine what you can improve and then practice a bit more.

Intro

If you pay attention, people say a version of "I don't feel like it" all the time. I don't feel like cooking, I don't feel like going out, I don't feel like going to work, I don't feel like doing laundry. I challenge you to really listen to what is being said in your world. Make a conscious effort to listen for the phrase, "I don't feel like it." Who is saying it? What are they saying it about? What do you think they are really saying? How does it make you feel?

There is this fantastical idea that when you own your business you will magically bounce out of bed everyday just chomping at the bit to get started. That you will be filled with such passion for your business that you will be tireless and inspired every single day.

Hahahahahahahahahahahahahahahahahahahahaha haha!

Buttercup, running a business is WORK. Yes, we both admit that there is a sense of "fire-in-your-belly" when it's your own. But guess what? You are still going to get tired, you still need to make very real sacrifices, and some days you are just not gonna wanna. And you have to. You have to do it anyway.

Liz

At the very core of all that I do is writing and as a writer at heart, I can relate to this idea of needing to be inspired. In 1934, Dorothea Brande wrote a brilliant book called *Becoming a Writer*. In it she dispels that idea that you need to be inspired to write. That is the romantic view of writing. But when you are in the content development business like I was for many years, you don't have the luxury of waiting around for a Muse. You have writing to do, so you do it. It isn't about "feeling like it", it's about discipline and commitment.

Ultimately your business is yours. You are going to make this business as much as you want it to be or as little as you want it to be. It certainly can fail if you allow it to and mental attitudes of "I don't feel like it" are a slippery slope to that statistical garbage can. Fifty percent of business owners make it past year five, fifty percent don't. Which one are you?

Buttercup, you don't have a boss anymore! There is no one who is going to come around and make sure you are doing what you need to do. Unless you have a killer admin, an excellent Project Coordinator, or you hire Accountability Coaches like us, you can get woefully behind really quick. Emails from clients asking, "What's going on?" are not fun, and if you are not careful, you can get trapped in a stressful spiral.

One of the baselines of being your own boss is being able to hold yourself accountable for the things that need to get done for your business. Now true, some days you just say there is nothing urgent going on and I'm going to take the afternoon off. A little free time off to get a pedicure or go fishing is an awesome bonus to a job well done. However, if you are still struggling to find clients and your revenues are not at goal, then not having a project is not the same as not having work.

You need time to work ON the business, not just IN the business. Working on the business means that back-office stuff like strategic planning, prospecting, marketing, sales, accounting, customer service, and customer loyalty. These are all the things you need to do to run and grow your business. That needs to happen whether you have a lot of clients keeping you working in the business, or not enough to keep you busy. And it can be fun!

I had a great coach a few years back tell me that whenever I wasn't in the mood or not feeling motivated, to just do the task for 15 minutes. To commit to whatever it was for 15 minutes. I found that after 15 minutes I was either miserable and hating it or I got into a groove and I could go another 15 minutes. If in the groove, well, problem solved, right? If miserable, I stopped, stepped away, and tried another 15 minutes a little later until I hit that groove.

Motivation can be like a train. It's hard to get going and pull out of the station, but once it is moving, it's moving! In fact, it then becomes hard to stop. It's necessary to find what it takes to get you up and going. Once you're moving, you're usually okay. This is different for every person. Maybe you need a list of your "whys". It could be your kids, your spouse, making money, the sports car you really want or maybe even being debt-free or financially independent. Keep your motivation front and center.

Some business owners respond well to a vision board that they create and look at during certain parts of the day or when they are feeling discouraged. You see the things you're working toward and can visualize your goals. Better yet, investigate your local networking organizations and join one that fits your personality and needs. There are leads groups, referrals groups, chambers of commerce, and organizations like ours, the KMA Network that has a mastermind and professional development focus. Get of out your head, talk to people, and you just might find yourself easing out of your slump.

Perhaps you need affirmations or some healthy self-talk to get your mindset in line. Building your business may not be thrilling every single moment, but every step you take moves you closer to your dreams. Keep your mind aligned to that end state and know that while there will be crappy days, there will also be amazing days. Maybe what will work is a phone call to a business mentor or colleague or Aunt Jo who can soothe you and inspire you. Or maybe you need to call someone who's not so soothing, someone who is going to be tough with you and say, "Suck It Up, Buttercup!" You know, someone a bit more like Tracie.

Tracie

"I don't feel like it" is the beginning of many statements with different endings. I don't feel like doing sales, I don't feel like cold calling, I don't feel like public speaking. Here is what I think "I don't feel like it" really is: "I am afraid." I am afraid of sales, I am afraid of cold calling, I am afraid of public speaking. I am afraid of putting myself out there, so I don't feel like it. It's become a good excuse for some business owners.

The whole "I just don't feel like doing that" often translates into I am afraid. It is very prevalent with public speaking. I see it in the networking world "I don't feel like speaking. I don't want to be the speaker. I am okay not speaking". Networking groups give you an opportunity to represent your business and to really tell people about what you do and why. It's an opportunity to show your passion and knowledge about your product or service and you don't feel like it? WHAT? It's a cheesy excuse. It really is "I am afraid to put myself out there because it's uncomfortable."

I know that public speaking is really uncomfortable for a lot of people. I can remember a time myself when I didn't like public speaking. These days public speaking is no big deal because it really isn't. I love what I do. I am passionate and knowledgeable about what I do. So, I have nothing to be afraid of.

Whether it's public speaking or through advertising means or social media, what is the best thing that could happen when speaking about your business? You get a new customer! What is the worst thing that could happen? Maybe someone asks a question you don't know the answer to? No problem. Say "I don't know the answer offhand but let me do some research. How can I contact you? I would love to get back to you with an answer". See? Problem solved. I really think fear, this low-level anxiety, needs to be knocked aside because the worst-case scenario for most things is so small.

I am a huge believer in analyzing the best and worst-case scenarios. When something I'm being challenged to do or I should do for my business makes me feel uncomfortable, I ask myself "What is the worst that could happen and what's the best outcome that can happen". Once I realize that the worst outcome isn't that bad, it is easy to do. In those rare occasions when it does seem like a bad outcome is possible, I tap into my network for support.

Here is a perfect example. I hate having my picture taken. I feel like most times I don't look good in pictures. I hate it. I hate when people want to take a candid snapshot. I hate the idea of having headshots done. Of course, it is a necessity for my business. I want to connect with people on a personal level, they need to see me.

When I think about worst case scenario, I know that it's possible that I will get an ugly picture. Guess what? I don't have to use it. What's the best-case scenario? I get an amazing picture and I can use the hell out of it. To make it easier, I get my hair and makeup professionally done so I can increase the chances of the most optimum outcome. Recently, I paid for professional headshots and a photoshoot. Yes, my accountability partner pushed the button and said we are doing this in 3 weeks and booked all the appointments photographer, hair and makeup. I was like, okay. The photographer was great, he took a ton of pictures. I didn't like all of them. There were a few I really loved. Guess what? I use them over and over and over again because they are great.

In my opinion there is another reason for the "I don't feel like it." Sometimes you just don't feel like it. Sometimes I don't feel like getting out of bed, and I suck it up. Occasionally I don't feel like making dinner, and I ask my husband to do it. There are times in our business where we don't feel like doing what we should. I don't feel like networking. Do you not feel like networking today? That is okay. Did you make a commitment to someone besides yourself to be there? No, then maybe you skip today and get back on track tomorrow. If instead you did make a commitment, then suck it up and go. If you don't feel like networking at all then you need to evaluate, what is that going to cost your business in the long run. Is there a way to get it done by someone else? Maybe you just need to suck it up and do it anyway.

What is really holding you back? Use the best case, worst case scenario analysis and squash the "I don't feel like it" and get it done. Can you hire someone to do what you don't feel like doing? If you have cut out or outsourced everything you don't feel like doing, and you still find that "I don't feel like it" is a constant in your business, maybe you should consider that what you don't feel like is owning and running a business.

Summary

The sense of "I don't feel like it" can have many sources. Maybe you are afraid, uncertain, unmotivated, or just plain lazy. Bottom line, you have to dig deep to figure out what is paralyzing you, solve it, and move beyond it.

This is your business, Buttercup. There is no Small Business Superman that is going to come out of the sky and make it all better. Get up, take a deep breath, phone a friend, and get moving. You are the only superhero in your world and making your business work from day-to-day is on you.

Yes, you can take a moment, perhaps even a day to step aside and reboot. If you are mindful of your commitments and client obligations, you can briefly step away and recharge. The key is to make sure you understand what is really going on and put solutions in place to avoid a repeat.

This is especially true if when you say, "I don't feel like it", you really mean "I am afraid". We get it, there are parts of being a business owner that are terrifying! Still, you need to move forward. You choose to walk through the figurative fire and come out stronger on the other side. So often, what scares us to paralysis really has very little downside. Take an objective view on the real worst-case scenarios, and then be brave.

Chapter 6: Mastermind Encouragement

Mastering frustration and fighting the urge to give up is an inside job. Take some time to reflect and recalibrate.

1. What are your grandest dreams for your company?
2. What scares you and how do you handle fear?
3. What is the worst that can happen?
4. What is the BEST that can happen?
5. Who can you call when you are stuck?
6. Can you take an afternoon or a day off to reboot?
7. Would you benefit from an accountability coach to keep you on track?

Intro

"I don't have time. There is no time for that. No one has any time. Time stands still for no man. I have all the time in the world for you. All in good time. Don't waste your time. Fall on rough times. In your spare time. Making up for lost time."

A whole book could be written on the clichés associated with time and it still wouldn't change a thing. Time after time people offer and accept "I don't have time" as a legitimate excuse in one way or another and it's about time that it changes.

Liz

Folks, let me just warn you here. This is one of Tracie's biggest pet peeves. When you get to her section, be prepared, because she is definitely going to tell you how it is. As for me, I see this in two different ways.

First, it's really never a matter of time. Everybody has the same amount of time in the day. I know it sounds cliché, but it's the truth. I understand that we all have different responsibilities and obligations in our daily lives, still we all get the same 24 hours in a day.

The real factor here is choice. What will you choose to do with your 24 hours? Will you plan ahead carefully balancing life and work? Will you overcommit and stress yourself out? Will you enlist support both at home and in your business or will you exhaust yourself trying to do too much? In the end, you are the commander of your calendar. Be judicious! Learn when to say no to distractions and when to say yes to taking care of yourself.

The second factor is energy. It's about managing more than time, it's also about managing how rested, healthy, and focused you are. You will come to realize that a constant theme in this book is that you must be willing to step outside your comfort zone to make your dreams come true.

When you own and operate your own business you are no longer building somebody else's dream. This is yours! You had the courage (or insanity) to become an entrepreneur, now you need to put in the time and effort to be a successful entrepreneur. If the price of that is giving up watching television every night, going to bed an hour earlier, or doing a little work on Saturday morning before everyone else wakes up, then so be it. This is for you!

If you are considering starting a business, make sure that you have family support. In the beginning, and maybe for a while after, there will be long days. There will be a lot of sweat equity and a lot of long hours to set the groundwork for your venture. For a while, your focus, time, and energy must shift to your business. You may think that you are Superman or Superwoman, but you are not. You will need help and you will need support.

I've seen talented professionals with a great business plan, launch businesses before making sure that they have the full support of the people in their daily lives. Spouses get resentful about having to pick up slack, kids complain that Mommy or Daddy works late, friends complain they never see you anymore, relatives don't understand what you are doing... The list goes on and it just creates stress and emotional drama. Launching a business has the potential to take you out of your normal routines for a while. If no one in your life wants to pitch in to take up the slack, then that is a recipe for disaster that no business model can cure or endure.

But what does this have to do with having enough time? We're getting there. Tracie and I have both encountered business owners in networking meetings that frequently express not having enough time to work on organizing and growing their business. But if you listen closely, they are recapping the latest episodes of multiple televisions shows. Hmmmm....

Please understand, television isn't evil. Personally, I'm a bit of Netflix binger (Any Stranger Things fans out there?) That said, I can assure you that I am not sacrificing time needed in my business to watch shows. People say that watching TV relaxes them, but does it really? I think it distracts you which isn't the same. You may feel like it's a mental break, but as soon as that show is over, all your worries and your to-do lists all come rushing back. Are you relaxed? Do you have peace of mind? What if instead of watching that show you had gone to bed earlier to be rested enough in the morning to get up earlier and tackle that list? Prioritizing becomes critical when you are running your own business.

Then you have the other extreme. I keep saying you need to be rested enough and some of you are wondering - what the heck is all that about? I know people who say there are lucky if they get four hours of sleep a night. I am going to suppress my urge to launch into a discussion about sleep deprivation in the United States (Google it!) and just say this: when you are sleep deprived, you typically have two states of being: Exhausted and highly caffeinated. Guess what, neither is a great mental state for solid decision making.

Running your own business is one of the greatest challenges you will ever take on in your life. You will invest your time, money, energy, and reputation into this business. Trying to do it sleep deprived is a really bad idea. You won't make good decisions, you won't be clear headed, and you are likely to be grumpy with the people that matter most like your partners and customers.

Yes, there are times when it is appropriate to burn the midnight oil, but this shouldn't be a lifestyle choice. Don't get sucked in to the myth that functioning on little sleep somehow makes you cooler or more invested than others. There is nothing smart about trying to run your business in zombie mode.

So be careful! Have a plan for how you're going to

stay healthy, how are you going to get enough rest, and who's going to be able to pitch in to take over anything in your life that you need to carve off to make time to be a business owner. Be willing to change things that you normally do. To have a successful business, you need more than a business plan. You need a matching life plan.

Tracie

"I don't have time" is my favorite worst excuse on the face of the earth. I read a quote one time on Facebook that I love it says, "I don't have time is the adult version of the dog ate my homework." It is totally true that every human being has 24 hours in a day, 7 days a week, 52 weeks in a year and what you do with that time is totally up to you. I cringe every time I hear one of the following statements:

- I don't have time to work *on* my business I am too busy working *in* my business.
- You don't understand how much it takes to run my business.
- I have a family, there is no time to take care of my business.
- There is not enough time to get it all done.
- My business shouldn't take all my time.

These are all excuses with solutions, but as long as you believe the excuses, then you won't ever change them.

Most entrepreneurs have to work on and work in their businesses, you have to set time aside for both. If you never take care of working on your business you will be working in your business until it fails. It doesn't matter what it takes to run your business, every business has needs. Build systems to make running your business easier and more efficient.

Many business owners have families and you need to find a balance between your business and family commitments. You may have to outsource some aspects of your business to free yourself up. Sure, you may feel like you can't get it all done, but if you start one piece at a time on the long list of tasks, you will be on your way. Your business shouldn't take up all your time, if it is, you need to evaluate why. Overall, the truth tends to be that you aren't lacking time, you are lacking systems.

You chose to run a business. I know a lot of people work for themselves because they got tired of working for someone else. They needed a better atmosphere, hated their boss, they could do it better, or needed more free time. These are all great benefits of owning your own business. Yet that flexible schedule and free time is not a given and it doesn't come right away. Sometimes we've got to suck it up and just do what needs to be done. Let's face it, if you have time to watch TV, go to bars, Facebook stalk, you have time to work on your business.

I am not saying every day, forever. There have been days in starting my business and in building my business where my day started at 5 am and I didn't get home until 9 o'clock at night. I barely had time to eat or pee because that's what it took to get the job done. You must make priorities. You need to choose today what is more important to you. What are the three things you need to get done for your business today? Ultimately, are you in your business to make money or is it more important to be up to date on "The Voice" or "Scandal" or whatever it is you're watching.

Through my kids' younger years, I always picked them up from school. That was something that was important to me and I almost always managed to make it happen. But I am not going to say that it was always easy. There were days that I had to sacrifice and say to myself I cannot pick them up today. I had to call Grandma, Grandpa, or an Aunt and see if someone else could pick them up because I had business commitments. It wasn't a regular thing though. I would say I was able to pick up my kids 99% of the time and have great memories of those times.

The 1% of the time when I couldn't pick them up, my kids really don't remember those days. They weren't left standing and waiting, I covered it, someone else did it. Usually they went and did something fun with them afterschool, the kids enjoyed it. It was like a little treat. This was not a punishment for them or me, the kids had a fun afternoon with family and I took care of business.

Sacrifices must be made. There is no such thing as you don't have time, the issue is that it wasn't important enough to you. What I encourage you to do every time you catch yourself saying or thinking "I don't have time" is to start over with "it's not important to me" and now tell me: do you not have time or did you just not prioritize your time? How important to you is it?

Real world example: A client once said, "I didn't have time to file my taxes." Really? All of January, February, March you couldn't find one afternoon to take care of it? Was it a surprise, did you not know that tax season was coming? You spoke to no one who grumbled about tax season? All throughout the year you had no idea that all those receipts were going to need to be dealt with? You had absolutely no free time for three whole months?

See the problem? I didn't have time to file my taxes really means filing my taxes was not important to me. These two statements make it really clear as to whether you had time or just wouldn't find the time. I think that when we change our mental stance or mental verbiage, it becomes clear. I didn't have time to watch American Idol or watching American Idol was not important to me. I can't make it any clearer.

Summary

Just as there is no such thing as "I don't have time". There is also no such thing as "you need to make time". We all have the same 24 hours in day. Just as we all have the choice of what we do with those hours.

Exchanging a corporate job for a running a business is often not an even swap. Maybe you will have more freedom, but be realistic and understand that you may also have more obligations. Resist the urge to wing it. You need to plan your time and be deliberate about balancing that hungry baby called "your business" with the needs of your family, friends, plus your own physical, mental, and spiritual health.

Prioritize, prioritize, and prioritize! Love to read but are finding it hard to sit with a book? Then switch to Audible and listen to books in the car to and from client meetings. Have a TV show you love? Digitally record it and watch when convenient without the commercials. Map out your needs, wants, and obligations and then schedule them intelligently.

Enlist help. Make sure you have a support system around you to pitch in when things get hairy (and they will). Even if you are an individual entrepreneur, the reality is that you never do it alone. Tap into your networking group, your mastermind partners, family, friends, coach, etc. Keep important people on "speed dial" and have a plan for the unexpected. Be proactive in creating balance in your schedule. This is your world now, and only you can keep it going long-term (so get some sleep!).

Chapter 7: Mastermind Encouragement

Time is finite and we cannot make more of it. Honestly, we can't even manage it, time flows no matter what we do. However, you can manage your behaviors and your choices about your activities.

1. List the things in your life that absolutely must be done by you.
2. List the things you don't need to do personally and list who can take over those duties while you focus on your business.
3. Define your work hours, leisure hours, and sleep hours.
4. Document anything that is sacred and non-negotiable such as time for church, going to your kid's games, morning yoga, date night, time with parents, etc.
5. Use this information to be realistic about your weekly calendar. Say "no" or "later" when necessary.

Intro

All throughout life there is always a moment where we don't know how to do something. As a baby you didn't know how to crawl. A little later you didn't know how to walk. As a young child you didn't know how to read. In the teenage years you didn't know how to drive. The list goes on and on. Even as adults we will still run into things we don't know how to do. The key to all this are the choices that you make when you run into something you don't know how to do.

Operating your own business requires constant learning and awareness. You need to keep up with skills, market trends, regulatory requirements, your network, etc. Business owners who stagnate often find themselves left behind. To grow over time you need to be agile and proactive about what you need to know to thrive. There is no employer or HR department sending you to training workshops or conferences. You have to take deliberate ownership of your professional development.

Liz

In my years as an entrepreneur some of my greatest jumps forward took place when I didn't know how to do something. Quite early in my freelance career a client asked me if I knew how to create forms on Microsoft Word. I knew that it could be done as I had played with it once before.

Since I felt confident I could figure it out, I said yes rather than no.

After all, if I couldn't figure out, I certainly could have found someone to teach me, or worst-case scenario, I could have outsourced the task. One way or the other, I could have delivered. In the end, I did figure it out and I kicked off a whole new service that enabled significant income over the years. All because I didn't shy away from something I didn't know how to do.

My willingness to say yes came from an experience I had years earlier when I was still in the corporate world. I was very fortunate to have a very brilliant boss, an executive by the name of Lori. Over the years she gave me positive feedback and built me up. Yet, the best feedback she ever gave me was the one time she had a heart-to-heart with me. She had asked me to create a special report on key performance indicators and I immediately started listing all the difficulties involved and how it was not really going to work. When I was done with my list of impossibilities, she looked at me and gently said, "Whenever I ask you for the impossible, you spend a lot of time and energy saying it can't be done and then you come back a few hours or a day later and you've got it figured out. So maybe instead of saying no you should just say yes from the beginning, or say 'let me see how I can figure that out'. That way you are not always saying no, especially since you always deliver."

She was right, I was constantly saying it couldn't be done, just to turn around and do it. I learned a big lesson that day. Even though I always delivered the product, I wasn't delivering a positive experience, not for my customer (in this case, my boss) or even for myself. Plus, I wasn't coming across as confident either! Thankfully, Lori believed in me and pushed me way outside of my comfort zone. After that conversation, I learned not to put up barriers because I didn't know how to do something. I learned the power of saying yes. Put that together with Jim Carrey's performance in *Yes Man* and I had a whole new perspective that was crucial to my success a few years later when I launched my own business.

Understand, I'm not suggesting that you take on things you cannot do. I am suggesting that you be open to expanding your world. Embrace learning new things and do not let fear keep you from making money. If you're going to be a business owner you have to be willing to go outside of your comfort zone, constantly!

If a client asked me if I could repair his copy machine, then my answer would have been "Let me refer someone who specializes in that." As best I can, I strive to never allow the answer to be "No." Ideally, I either can do the work, or I can refer someone who can. That way I am always a valuable resource.

The key to this whole "I don't know how" is not a basket of skills. It's courage. It's about being brave enough to understand that if clients are consistently asking for XYZ, it may behoove you to go learn how to do XYZ. It might be scary, but you know what? Knowledge has a way of reducing big scary things to silly things, even exciting things.

Do you remember learning how to ride a bike? There was never a good explanation about what exactly you needed to do to keep those two wheels upright (except, pedal, pedal, keep pedaling – thank you grandpa!). Still, once you got the feel of riding your bike, you wanted nothing to do with those training wheels again. You were a big boy or girl and you were moving on to wheelies!

These days you can learn to do just about anything. Seriously, if it's not on YouTube, there are probably 100 online webinars, many local workshops, and at least once person in your extended network that teaches whatever you need to learn. You just need to be brave enough to do it. Take the time and spend the money to invest in yourself. I see people complain about the cost of workshops and certification programs, and that always puzzles me. Knowledge is forever. If that training is going to augment your skills and enable greater revenues then it's not a cost, it's an investment. Stop whining about investing in your future and figure out how to make it happen.

I had a unique opportunity to invest in myself by coaching with Lisa Nichols. You may remember her as one of the teachers in the movie "The Secret" years ago. Since then, Lisa has evolved to be an international speaker and masterfully leads a multi-million dollar coaching organization. I spent a significant chunk of money to participate in her program. Not only was it worth every penny, but I never really saw it as me paying Lisa. I saw it as investing in myself.

You see, people get stuck on giving their money to other people, especially if they think that person already has a lot of money. It's a mindset pitfall, a broke mentality side-effect that keeps people from stepping up. So what if Lisa makes millions of dollars a year? Good for her! I never resent anyone's abundance. On the contrary, successful people show us what is possible for us. So, get over the hesitation. It doesn't matter who you pay, if the knowledge is valuable and you put it to good use, what you have done is invest in yourself, and you are absolutely worth it!

Tracie

"I don't know how". First let me say no one knows how to do everything. No one is expected to know it all. Suck It Up, Buttercup is about getting rid of the excuses that are preventing you from succeeding in business and "I don't know how" is just that, an excuse.

I don't know how to do marketing, sales, social media, file my state taxes. How lazy can you be? Really you don't know how? The internet, the internet is a wonderful thing! You can look up and learn just about anything. Okay, so you can't trust that everything on the internet is true or right but you have options. There are so many ways to get help. Ask another business owner, do you file state sales tax? How do you do it? Can you show me how? Can you teach me?

Ask a professional like your accountant to show you

or pay them to take care of it for you. If you don't know how to do sales, don't worry there are a million books or YouTube videos that can help you. Take a class on sales. Ask someone you know who is great at sales: Can I role play with you? Can I take you to lunch and pick your brain about sales? That's a straightforward way to do it. Get a sales coach and really delve into what works best for you.

"I don't know how" is really "I didn't take the time to find out how." In this day and age there is no reason to not know how to do something that is vital to your business. No reason at all.

Personally, I didn't know how to do sales when I first started personal training. I didn't even know it was a sales job. Which was evident to my manager. When my manager asked me why I wasn't closing sales at a comparable ratio to the rest of the team, my answer was "what is a closing rate?" I didn't realize sales was part of personal training. I was hired to teach people how to work out, I wasn't hired as a sales person, right?

I had never been trained in sales and had never worked in a sales position. Prior to personal training I was working as a house painter before that I was in the military, no sales involved. I went to business school and learned how to run a business, but I never learned to sell. As a Personal Trainer, I was paid a small hourly fee to work the floor but my paycheck was primarily commissions from the sale of personal training packages.

The manager said "Why don't you meet with Jane,

she is our top sales person at the gym." So I met with Jane for a couple of weeks and she enlightened me on how she did her sales. I started implementing what I learned and I was off and running. Once I learned that I had a sales job and learned some sales techniques I saw my paycheck climb. The learning didn't stop there. I make it a point to watch and listen to others when they are selling and I take notice of what I do and don't like as continuing education for myself. I read books and take seminars on sales too.

Right now you might be thinking "I don't have time to learn." That's right, I know you are tempted to combine these two excuses. STOP! You don't have time to learn or is learning not important to you? Now you might be thinking, "I don't want to learn another thing." STOP!

Let's work through this together with an example about bookkeeping. You might be thinking you don't have time to learn bookkeeping. Or you might be thinking you don't want to learn bookkeeping. The first solution is to make it a priority to learn basic bookkeeping. The other solution is hire a bookkeeper. Bookkeeping still needs to get done. If bookkeeping isn't done your business will suffer. Your business could even fail because you don't know the numbers in your profit and loss report or didn't properly file your taxes as a result of not doing your bookkeeping.

Not knowing how and not taking care of vital business processes just makes it more likely your business will not be celebrating a fifth anniversary. In the real world, "I don't know how" has two simple answers. Make it a priority to learn or make enough money to pay someone who already knows how. If you don't feel like you have the budget to outsource, then schedule time on your calendar, get over your fears, and start learning.

Summary

One of the neat side effects of the digital explosion of the past decade is the increasing access to knowledge. If you live in a country with reliable internet access, you can pretty much learn anything you want. Now certainly, many things like brain surgery and rocket science, are going to involve some hands-on education.

It is equally valid to say that so much of what you need to know to successfully run a business can be learned from the internet, books, peers, industry leaders, mentors, and coaches. Whether its business management or industry-specific skills, the world is pretty much at your feet. You just have to embrace the learning process.

Let's say you set out to learn a subject and discovered you either hated it or were just awful at it. That knowledge is important, especially if that is a skill your clients expect from your business. If you can learn it, it's a win! If you can't, then you know you need to hire it internally or outsource externally.

When you confront what you don't know and make honest attempts at learning, you are evolving your business in a positive way. Sure, it may be hard, but that is never an excuse. You've read this chapter after chapter: Be brave, Buttercup! You are the ultimate champion of your business. Fear is not an option! If there is something you need to learn, find a way, invest in yourself, and bravely take action!

Chapter 8: Mastermind Encouragement

In this information age, you can learn pretty much anything you want to learn. Take the time to plan your professional development. After all, knowledge is forever.

1. What have you always wanted to learn but haven't yet?
2. What is a developing trend in your industry that will require you to learn new skills? What is your plan of action to stay informed?
3. How do you prefer to learn?
4. What organization or person can you access to learn the way you like to learn?
5. Build a plan, with dates and budgets, outlining when you will develop the skills you need and want. Make a commitment – share it with a mentor or coach.

Intro

In an ideal world no one would ever get sick or injured. Unfortunately, in the real-world illness and injury are a fact of life. As an entrepreneur and a business owner the question isn't "Will you have to deal with getting sick or injured?" The question is "How does your business function and survive when you get sick or injured?"

Liz

When you are sick, take the day off. Work when you are better.

Oh, I so want that to be my final answer! I really do…but alas! That is not usually the life of a business owner. Depending on the status of my projects, there are times when I can accommodate a day of feeling under the weather and my client's never need to know. Other times, I have to reach out and negotiate deadlines. Life happens and most of the time clients are very understanding.

What do you do when you need to curl up in bed but the work must go on? The best thing to do is to have a short-term and long-term plan. Short-term relates to covering a few days or maybe a couple of weeks while you recover from the flu or some short period of convalesce. Long term addresses what happens if you need to address an illness or injury that is going to take you out of pocket for several weeks or months.

Two strategies that can resolve short and long-term absences from your business involve *automation* and *delegation*. Based on your specific situation, you need to determine if you can punt parts of your business to others or if you need to temporarily shut down operations. What this looks like varies greatly depending on your business model. Businesses that are primarily based on passive income are easier to step away from than a business where you are the primary product.

If you're an author and people simply buy and download your books, being sick for a few days or even a few weeks may be completely irrelevant to your ability to produce income. On the other hand if you are a mechanic in a one-man shop, your income may be completely shut down until you are well enough to work. Understanding how an absence from your business impacts your income stream is critical and I urge you to plan ahead.

What can you automate? Are there any functions in your business that you can spend a little time automating so you have more time to rest and recover? Consider setting up an auto responder in your email service to let people know when you will respond. If you have an active social media presence and don't want that to falter, schedule your posts for the next several days. Use scheduling options directly in the social network platform or use a post scheduler such as Hootsuite or Sprout.

If clients typically need certain information from you, can you create a quick FAQ list on your website or perhaps a PDF document to email? While this may be overkill if you have a cold for a day or two, it may be valuable if you need a week or two away from your business.

What can you delegate? Do you have an assistant, local or virtual, that can take up the slack while you are recovering? Do you have a team that can step in? Have you trained and tested scenarios where you put them in charge? Every major company in the world has a Business Continuity Plan. Being a small business doesn't mean that you get to ignore taking these same preparations. Sony can probably absorb the loss if a department is shut down for a day. Can you?

If you don't have an internal team to whom you can delegate operations while you are out sick, then think outside the box. Is there someone in your network or mastermind group that can step in? Within our KMA Network, we've had members do dishes at busy restaurants, answer phones, deliver products, etc. Members collaborate with each other to keep businesses going. How about this, do you have good relationships with a trusted competitor? Wait, before you say that sounds insane, let me explain.

Years ago, I stepped away from a networking group while I took long-term project. When I returned a few months later, I noticed a strange vibe. Turns out that while I was away, another resume writer had joined the group. The group leaders were thrilled to know that I welcomed the new member. In a nation of millions of adult professionals, there is plenty of work for many resume writers. I'm a big believer in collaboration over mindless competition.

Before I could reach out, the new member contacted me and asked to meet. I agreed and we had a GREAT conversation. It turned out that our styles are similar, we have the same ethical approach to our process, and pricing is fairly in line. Many years later, we still enjoy a great relationship. When I am on vacation or when I had wrist surgery (don't worry, it wasn't carpal tunnel, just an encounter with a stubborn window), I routed clients to her. She in turn, sent me a referral fee for each client I directed to her. While I wasn't making 100% of my income, at least potential clients weren't hitting a dead-end and I had a stream of passive income coming in. When she is busy or on vacation, she refers her clients to me. It's mutually beneficial.

The best time to look for solutions to downtime is before anything happens. Carefully analyze scenarios that may put you in the position to be absent from your business. Certain scenarios can be serious such as a complicated surgery with a long recovery period or you being displaced by a natural disaster. Investigate how to mitigate the risks. I won't go deep into this, but also consider purchasing disability or disaster insurance to offset your loss of income.

Tracie

Let me start by saying that YOU decided to open your

own business. As owners, there are no sick days, paid vacation, or paid time off. You will get sick. You will go on vacation. You will need time off. Have you stopped to think about what happens when you are sick? Do you have a plan? The world doesn't stop just because you are sick and neither does your business.

Scenario one: "I woke up this morning and I feel yucky. Nothing really wrong, but ugh, I just can't. Oh well, I will just roll over and go back to sleep. After all, I need my rest. I am sick!" I don't think so, Buttercup! Your customers and your business deserve consistency and can't be ignored because today you are sick. If you are just feeling yucky but you are presentable and are not in any way contagious, then suck it up and take care of your business. Whatever you do don't complain all day about how you don't feel good to your customers, they don't want to feel like they have inconvenienced you or feel guilty about how you are feeling. If you don't like how that feels, then develop a plan so that you don't have to experience this again in the future, like an employee that can run things for you.

Scenario Two: "I woke up, I'm sick, coughing, sneezing, fever but I am going to work anyway because without me the business can't run." Hell, no Buttercup. Don't share whatever crap it is you have, no one wants to catch it. Your customers, employees, and vendors will not appreciate you sharing your germs. I understand you may be essential or in some cases you are the business and without you it really doesn't run but that does not make it okay to come to work sick and contagious. If you are the business, you should have a plan for when you get sick in a yucky, contagious way.

There should be a budget buffer that takes into account that you may be out sick at least a few days occasionally. Make sure that you can contact clients, customers or anyone you would need to interact with to let them know that you will need to reschedule or delay. Most people understand that illness and accidents happen and as a small business you may not have the manpower to make appointments or meet project deadlines if you are ill or injured. You must, and I mean it, you must communicate. Being sick is not an excuse to not communicate. You can't just blow off your responsibilities no matter how sick you are. Not letting a customer know what is going on will only compound the situation.

Let me put this a different way. If you are a parent of children or fur babies you have responsibilities. These babies need things from you on a daily basis and there is really no day off. Children and pets need attention, food and their bathroom needs met regularly. As a parent when you are sick do your babies not eat? Of course, they do, you either suck it up and do it yourself or if you are that sick you make arrangements for someone else to take care of their needs. Your business is just like your child or fur baby, it is your business baby. Just like your other babies it needs constant attention and care in order to thrive. So, you should have a plan for your business baby for times of illness or accidents so that your business continues to thrive and love you back with profits.

Summary

Your health is important and we do not in any way advocate ignoring your health. That said, you need to be very mindful of what sick means now that you are a business owner. Non-contagious allergies that make you feel run-down but are temporary are not a great reason to shut down. A highly infectious disease that makes green stuff come out of your facial orifices should keep you from public appearances, but maybe you can still answer emails. Serious surgery is obviously going to keep you out of pocket for a few days or a few months.

Make a plan now. Don't wait until you don't feel well or worse until a catastrophic health crisis takes place. All companies need a business continuity plan and one of the events that triggers that plan is illness. You need to have a step-by-step road map of what to do when your ability to produce income is compromised.

Be proactive in mapping out how and when clients get notified that projects may be slightly delayed, placed on hold, or stopped altogether. In certain circumstances you will do this yourself, but you need to have a clear plan of action when you are too ill (or unconscious) to do this yourself. Even as a solopreneur you need a trusted back-up person that can access your communication platform and let customers know what to expect.

Protecting your business is your responsibility. You

may feel healthy as a horse today. Maybe you are one of those lucky ducks that "never gets sick". Still, you need to plan for any kind of emergency absence that may disrupt your income stream and your service to your clients. Preserving the integrity of your brand is critical to long-term success, so suck it up when you can, and use your continuity plan when you must.

Chapter 9: Mastermind Encouragement

Accidents and injuries can take you out of commission on a temporary basis, but with proper planning, they don't have to destroy your business. Take the time to safeguard your processes and your income.

1. List one or two trusted people in your life who will have access to your business accounts if you are indisposed. Make sure they know what to do.
2. Create a business continuity plan. This doesn't have to be a 3-Inch binder in small print. Even a checklist of "what do to if" will be invaluable if you find yourself unable to lead your business.
3. Document your disability and insurance coverage and make sure your spouse, dependents, or power-of-attorney holder has access to the policies.
4. Explore strategic partnerships or referral agreements that allow you to route prospects and clients when you are either too busy, sick, or otherwise just not available.

Intro

We all have days when we thinking to ourselves "I am so over this!" The key is knowing if you are experiencing temporary frustration or is it time to enact your exit strategy.

Regardless of who you are or what your business is, that day will come. The day that you know at the very core of your being that you don't want to do this anymore. How you get there may vary. Maybe your business is hugely successful and has given you financial freedom so you just don't want to do it anymore and you don't need to. You may have found that you have grown as an individual and a business person so it is time for you to move on to bigger and better things. There is also the possibility that your business is a drain on you and your resources and it is time to get out. All businesses need an exit strategy.

Liz

Through the years I've had client's come to me and say those words that are hard to hear "I don't want to do this anymore". I have a confession, I said those words too. Right around year five in my business, my primary client was affected by new regulations in his industry. Rather than reinvent himself, he decided to close shop.

That left me in the position of having to find one or more clients to replace his income. I had recently been through a major upheaval in my personal life and just couldn't find the energy to climb that mountain. Instead, I polished my resume and put it "out there".

Within two weeks I had a GREAT job offer. Huge salary, nice title, my own office, an admin....AN ADMIN! Woo-Hoo, I hit the jackpot, right? Well, in many ways I did. I met amazing people. Incredible professionals who had gumption, vision, and deep commitment to their roles. Six months later, I gave my notice.

I had been successful in my role and was thankfully well-liked in the organization. The problem? My passion didn't match the long hours. I had no work-life balance and that was really important to me. The level of leadership I held in this organization demanded a sacrifice I didn't have in me to give. I realized then and there that if I was going to work those hours, I was going to do it for my own business.

I relaunched my business and it has skyrocketed since then. Why? Because I knew that I was ruined for corporate work. The idea of "I can always get a job" if my business didn't pan out was gone. I didn't love my Plan B, so my Plan A HAS to work. I need to know that the work I do is directly impacting the lives of others in a meaningful way and frankly, I want to set my own pace and my own hours.

Once I returned to my business and let go of any back-up plans, I was all in. Everything aligned. Before I could even get my marketing "machine" going, I started getting calls out of the blue from prior clients and referrals started pouring in. My revenues have grown in double digits year-over-year since then. It all flowed and I believe that was a direct result of my level of commitment.

So, the question I have for you is…. are you committed?

If the answer is yes, then you just need the right support, knowledge, skills, and maybe coaching to make sure you are actively growing your business every day. If the answer is no, then it's time to make decisions and enact your exit strategy.

Ideally, you started with the end in mind and already know your exit strategy. What I mean is this, a business owner who wants to sell their business when they are ready to retire needs to build and operate their business in a way that makes their assets transferable.

Conversely, an owner who "is the business" and plans to simply close up shop when they are done, can have a very different business model. If you are not sure how you are set up or how you want to exit the business, consider speaking to your CPA, attorney, and possibly even a business broker. Before you walk away, be sure to understand your options and exit your business in the most lucrative manner with low risk and no ongoing liability for the business operations.

Finally, make sure you are truly emotionally ready to let go. Once you sell or close that business, there is no going back. Okay, maybe you can resurrect a closed business, but in many ways you will be starting over. If you are absolutely, mentally, emotionally, and financially ready to retire or move on to something different, then do it. I'm a big believer in reinvention. Start your new phase with joy and enthusiasm. I congratulate you and wish you all the best!

Tracie

I don't wanna work. I don't wanna get up. I don't wanna struggle. I don't wanna keep this going. Stop whining!

Is it that you don't wanna do this anymore? Are you just having a moment? Or is it time to say good bye to your business? All three of these are okay, yet need to be handled differently. A business should be your passion and you should have some emotional connection to it. When that starts to fade, you really need to look at why.

Are you just having a moment? Yes, even people completely in love with their businesses have moments in time where they find themselves wondering why. Why am I doing this? I am done! I have seen this many times with business owners that I network and socialize with. I have even had those moments myself. Even when we are completely in love with our business, we don't always like it (just like with our spouse or kids).

Sometimes you have a bad day, week, month, year at work just like everyone else. When I feel like this, I find it helpful to take some time off. A mental health day. Just relax. After relaxing, the moment passes and I can get back to the joy of being a business owner.

Lunch is a great way to work through the moments of "why am I doing this"? Yes, I said lunch. Have lunch with trusted business owners or a mentor and vent the frustrations of being in business. I have had lunches like this with other business owners and once they see that they are not alone, it gets better. The moment is not so permanent and scary.

Are you overwhelmed by processes or the day-to-day operations? That can be fixed if you still have the fire burning for your business. Take some time and evaluate which parts of your business are weighing you down. Once you know what parts are weighing you down, then you need to evaluate again. You need to figure out why they are weighing you down. There are parts of a business that are draining. If you know how to do the work required but doing it drains all the passion and drive out of you, then hire someone to do it for you.

Another reason owners feel drained is a lack of systems. Everything always seems to be in chaos and the list of things to do keeps growing and nothing seems to be improving. Building systems is a lot of work and can be overwhelming, so enlist help. Get an accountability partner or a coach to help you through the process and keep it on track. You will feel much better when it's done.

Whether you develop the systems you need to manage your business better or hire someone to take those soul crushing tasks off your plate, both solutions let you get back to what you love most about your business.

Now don't get me wrong, the answer isn't always to stay. It really isn't good for a business when the owner really doesn't want to be there anymore. If that is where you are, for whatever reason, there is definitely something you can do, you can sell. That's right sell your business and move on! Don't stay in the "unhappy marriage for the sake of the kids." If you are truly unhappy, the business will suffer. Get out while the getting is good and the business can be sold.

I believe people are reluctant to get out because they feel like it is admitting defeat or giving up on the dream. There is no defeat in knowing when your time is up. It's not giving up on the dream but it is an opportunity to pursue a new dream; a dream that fires you up and has you excited about getting up and building your business. Go for it!

Summary

Every business has its last day. Well, unless you are the Old Farmer's Almanac in print since 1792. Most businesses have a last day. With focus, strategy, the right team, and a sensible business model your business will ideally end when you choose for it to end. If you are feeling like you don't want to do this anymore, you need to assess whether you need a day off, a vacation, or if it's time to put your exit plan in motion.

As business owners we spend countless hours

thinking of more ways to grow the business, to expand, and to sell, sell, sell. But what happens the day you wake up and know, deep in your core, that you are done?

If you are have properly planned, you have an exit plan in place. If you don't have one yet, we encourage you to plan the end of your business with as much fervor and enthusiasm as you planned the launch of your business. Every business deserves a well thought out exit plan. Will you retire and close the business? Sell the business for profit? Leave it to your kids?

How you intend for your business to end also greatly shapes how you grow your business. Don't wait until you are burnt out, bored, or rolling in so much money that you want to abandon what you spent so long building. Make a plan and be proactive in keeping a pulse in your commitment to the business. Ending your time as a business owner can be a joyous (and profitable) retirement or a painful and costly demolishing of everything you created. In the end, Buttercup, you decide what your company's eulogy will say. Make it a good one.

Chapter 10: Mastermind Encouragement

Someday, it will be time to move on from your business. Preparing now gives you a better chance of exiting your business on your own terms.

1. Take some time to consider, how long you have been

feeling that you "don't want to do this anymore"?
2. Is it a fleeting sense of discouragement or are you feeling an urgent need to walk away?
3. Schedule a chat in a private place with someone you trust. This may be an emotional conversation, so be sure you have the privacy to express yourself.
4. Go on vacation. Unplug and get some distance from the business. Having time to think outside of daily pressures may add valuable perspectives.
5. Consider what you need to change to be in love with the business again. Are you willing to make those changes and carry forward?
6. Review your exit plan. Talk with your accountant, attorney, and perhaps a business broker. Can you retire comfortably? Sell the business profitably? Leave it to an heir? Know your options before you make decisions.

In this book we have discussed ten common excuses that we have seen keep business owners from thriving. You may not identify with all of them but throughout a business lifetime you may briefly experience all of them.

Feeling, saying, or experiencing some of these situations does not make you a bad business owner, it makes you human. What you do when you're being sucked in by excuses is what determines if you will be a long term business owner or another sad statistic. Will you take focused action? Will you hold yourself fiercely accountable?

Our goal in writing this book was to shake you up. Complacency and "good-enough" are dangerous conditions that keep good businesses from being great. A limiting mindset or skill-set can create self-imposed barriers that keep you cut-off from the success you really want.

Through Suck It Up, Buttercup, we aim to wake-up business owners like you so you can switch from a downward spiral to an upward momentum. Sometimes our words may seem harsh, they aren't meant to be. Still, keep in mind that reality can feel harsh and nice words don't always get the job done.

In planning this book, we knew that showing you barriers that are keeping you stuck would not be enough. Recognizing your excuses is a good first step but it can leave you feeling overwhelmed. That is why we included actions steps at the end of every chapter. In our KMA Network, we give our members Mastermind Encouragements every single week.

In this book, every chapter has a Mastermind Encouragement section. We showed you the barriers, then we gave you clear actions that build a path forward. Beyond feeling empowered, we want you to actually BE empowered. Action, Buttercup, defined and sustained action, will take you and your business to phenomenal levels of success. If you want to go further with the action steps, we invite you to visit https://kmanetwork.com/buttercup-workbook to download the official companion workbook. It's available to all our readers at no additional cost.

Maybe you are ready to make a commitment, to blast away excuses, but are not sure if you can do it on your own. We understand, change can feel scary, especially when you are trying to overcome challenges that are of your own doing. Changing our own behaviors and habits can be tough.

Our advice is simple, either find a steadfast accountability partner or hire a business coach. If you chose an accountability partner, give them this book to read, then have an honest discussion about which one (or a few) of the 10 excuses are hindering your success. Prioritize the excuses you want to tackle, write a clear plan for overcoming the excuses, and set specific methods for measuring success and checking in with each other.

If you prefer to work with a business coach, we invite you to learn more about our Mastermind-Based coaching programs. We offer multiple programs and work with professionals, entrepreneurs, business owners, and corporate groups all over the United States. Keystone Mastermind Alliance coaching programs feature:

Fierce Accountability - designed for clients who already know what needs to be done and want to be held accountable for consistent and timely action. We give you a personal layout of tasks with priority, action steps, and fierce commitments which we monitor on a weekly basis using a custom board on Trello (a very cool online program).

Achievement Coaching - the next level in KMA coaching includes 2 on 1 coaching with Liz M. Lopez & Tracie Thompson. The purpose is to develop clarity, set goals, plan business growth, identify and overcome challenges – all in a structured environment that promotes a positive focus on action and accountability. You can book a one-time consultation or packages for multiple sessions.

Badass Business Coaching – this six month coaching intensive starts with the basics and ramps up to uncover your purpose, develop a clear action plan, and gives you the mindset and skillset to achieve greatness. It is a complete A through Z business deep dive. Sessions can be intense (yet supportive) and we take accountability seriously!

If you would like to work with us, please visit https://kmanetwork.com/business-coaching to review options and submit a request for coaching services. Our team will reach out within two business days to explore the best coaching program to boost your success.

Now, Get to Work Buttercup!

Thank you for taking the time to read this book. We hope it has shocked you, moved you, and inspired you to **BIG BOLD** action. If you found it valuable, then please leave us a great review on Amazon, then stop messing around get to work on growing your business, no excuses! Your success lies on the other side of your action.

Made in the USA
Columbia, SC
12 May 2019